I0111640

MIXTAPE / VOL 3 / THE NEW POOR MANUAL FOR THE LIVING /

JUSTIN DAVID KOONTZ
JOSHUA ROBERT LONG

ISBN-13: 978-0692534281
ISBN-10: 0692534288

1st Edition Printing

This book features the editorial work of The Legal Endowment For Wednesday Night Activities.

Cover design by Robert High
Hands and two dollar bills by Corey Green

For addition titles or information on The Mixtape Series, please visit *SOCKRIDES.COM*

MIXTAPE / VOLUME 3 / THE NEW POOR MANUAL FOR THE LIVING /

JUSTIN DAVID KOONTZ
JOSHUA ROBERT LONG

14 September 2015

Just as we were putting the finishing touches on this book, a beloved member of our small community lost his life. His name was Toby and he was a gray and white cat that was born in Oregon almost ten years ago. He traveled here to Ohio in a van with my wife and her ex-boyfriend when she moved here for college almost seven years ago. I met him when my wife and I were just friends and she was living up in Hiram, Ohio, doing a little stint at the college up there. There was something about his attitude that just immediately gravitated towards myself. Others who happened to meet him saw it too, even strangers across the worldwide internet. Around the ninth of September, he began acting very suspicious. He was throwing up a lot and generally just seemed to have no interest in anything except sleeping behind the couch. On September twelfth, my wife asked me to assess his condition when I came home from work and figure out if he should go to the vet. Three days just seemed like too long of a time to be that sick, and she worried something was more seriously wrong with him.

I took him to the vet when I got home, and we found out a couple hours later that he had diabetes and that had been what made him suddenly so ill. Something he ate just set it off, and he was basically on a one-way trip to diabetic coma town USA. The vet seemed fairly confident that he would be a-okay and was treating him with a variety of things. As the night went on, my wife and I were lying around on the couch watching Netflix when the phone rang. It was the vet again. Her voice sounded exactly opposite to the tone she had when she called earlier. She informed me that Toby had just passed away minutes prior to the call. Shell-shocked a bit, my wife and I immediately hopped in the car and went to spend a few minutes with him. It was the most devastating afternoon and evening I had since the passing of my mother. And I know some of you reading this probably think that is strange, that he was only a cat, etcetera. But it blew my heart apart.

Here in the aftermath of that, Justin and I just wanted to point out that everything you read in the pages of this book, and the very fact that you're holding it at all—it's all because of and dedicated to the memory of the guy known as The Tube Man, Flappy Pappy, Tubs, and whatever else you knew him as.

Toby we love you little dude. And we hope wherever you are, there's a bit of peace and a few little bits of popcorn for you to chew on, and maybe, just maybe a water fountain.

Dear Cottage: You Ruined My Fucking Life

(here are the floors of the cottage,
here are the basement songs).
Here are last year's tomatoes,
here are the beers from the market-
on the tables
on the floors

I've shined them for you.

The coffee stains the stove
and the wine stains my lips
and the cigarettes stain my teeth
the mold clings to my lungs
and we're all afraid of the bathroom.

Here, we've all been made.

Here are the next show's stickers,
there on the table by the drill;
there where Loren fell in the mop/bucket
and where Sedona punched the stranger down to the throat .

where is the case hidden?
where do the lighters go?
where are the keys?
who is the next big thing for all of us here in saturday's lamp/shade lime-light.

Here on the couch,
under the bookshelf
-by the merch booth
-by the door
-in the way.

Who painted this?
Who's got a pick stashed away?
who dropped the drugs?
how did the organ break?
How did we get home?
Who brought the assholes?
Who grabbed my bike?

Who is going to clean the goddamned bathroom?

I Caught On Fire In The Office

I grabbed two clementines out of the bowl
by the secretary on my way out

The mirrored steel of the elevator showed
my red orange blue brilliance as I wiped another
clump of ash from my forehead

Pushing the button for the bottom floor
I realized how my keys were still just sitting
on my desk

The older gentleman at the security desk gave me
the side-eye as I breezed through the revolving door

The breeze felt comfortable against my own heat
as my shoes began to stick to the sidewalk which
was counting each step

> There is a strange sense in following my old
> trail home   The muck of ash
> going up Long's Hill and turning right onto
> Spencer It was as if I had never left
> or could never figure out a shorter way to
> just make it all seem so over with

From The Tacoma

There's a dim-lit renaissance nightclub
in the southwest alleys of hell,
the scene feels like the arid empty
of the Catalina foothills
-the living dead time lapse
of all that drooping cancerous foliage.

Somewhere there's a Cello,
someone sings a song.

The night smells blue-grey
and feels like bruised skin
right on the nape of the neck

like being kissed by a hammer.

There are children laughing over yellow lines on world maps,
tracing with stick-jam fingers where the bombs have sailed.

Night bars and broken windows singing

and it's home,
somewhere it's home.

A Forgone Conclusion / Bulldozing An Afternoon

You find yourself giving head at two in the afternoon,
then slicing cheese sandwiches in half with a butter
knife.

> Youth finds that dishes come—and—go—that
> couches retain the previous afternoon almost
> as well as your neighbor's memory. He filed a
> noise complaint that one time, and Martin was
> outside being broken glass obnoxious as he
> and a bottle became separated. For two hours
> he made it seem like he cleaned himself up
> until the following morning the neighbor sprawled
> in chalk on the porch that IF YOU BROKE GLASS
> YOU NEED TO CLEAN IT UP.

Youth taught me that dressing yourself up only makes
the touching you will end up doing more inert. It will then
make you spend fifteen years drowning yourself in the
toilet until your desire learns how to forget. A friend told
me that my view was such a disjointed take on the
office, but it was hard to take him seriously when he
was pressing his feet into my head.

Doom, LEFT DOOM

The most thrilling
and upsetting thing
I can possibly fathom

is one-million white faces DOOMED to HELL
for crimes against hu[man]ity

and while heaven exists as a multicultural Paradiso
of old worship
    and celebrations .

ALL US LEFTISTS scream from the fiery pits
still aimed at de-centralization,

while the ideological & mighty institution
plays power-grab amidst the demonic legions
claiming that darkness had always been the way
(and secretly they had known all along).

WE SMILING ANARCHISTS
cast to the inner cities of the inferno
looking for a locally grown co-op
and bumming stogies from sharp-toothed devils
dancing and singing all the while.

We're incessantly muttering

"we could really clean this place up"
all the while chanting

        DON'T GIVE EM HELL!

in the downtown-
frozen lake protests
face to face
with old Diablo himself.

"i've always loved you as Pan"
we'll say

"but don't turn your back to the working class,
everyone deserves their fair share of damnation,

-and they truly do.

I Was Standing Behind A Car After I Got Married

It was something less than forty hours
or so, the planes had already hit the skies
        above me, though aside from that,
        the day tasted and looked just
        as great as the night before

The stranger that turns into a kiss that turns
into the hand of fate, and suddenly you're
burning down churches and rosebushes and
rusted jars of nails that you once used to
hang shit artwork that your friends had painted

I was standing behind a car
        looking at her as
she was taking my photograph,
all-at-once a dream in sequence,
her—my wild sidecar—the ache
and the solution, which is all
inspiration should ever consist of—

and she was mine and the fire and the moon reflecting into the dirt

Response to the Bones

They spoke of our generation(s)
in bittersweet tongues, steel-cooled and poured over by our years
stacked
earth upon earth upon earth above some.

I promised that the lines in the trees wore our truths
and half-lives.

The problem remained
in their absence.

When the shots were fired between avenues
when the knives were drawn under flicker'd lights.

Here is the new dialogue they've been asking for,
tic typed in windowpane sunlight.

WE were born here on the center ground
                    rolling out
toward the edges of absolute zero;

in possibility

 in hate

 in grief

 in hope

      in gravity: the equalizer.

They weren't there for the new sun rising
over the steam of the last god-forsaken wars

and the absences at the ballot box-

and all of it's
feigned interest
 between the same tides
 weaving back over
every four years.

We weren't all retreating to the woods with
hands tied,
we didn't need the badge of honor.   *13*

we didn't crucify the nine-to-five

or find a way around it.

we've been fixing the shelves where our ideas lay

we were fighting all our own,
because the neurons fired,
and we were huddled in the maze,

looking out;

just like them.

The Earth That Sank The Rain

They didn't drink so much as
            they just danced
foot over foot—
            A simmering sinkhole
of sunken faces, not enough
bones between them to laugh—

The sentiment was there, smiling,
            on the television—they mentioned
                        there would be an alarm sounding—
but it was over as soon as it began

All of them sunken into the Earth

Birds began to trollop across the lines
of fencing, each one tilting their head
attempting to better understand
these new valleys that appeared
beside the sidewalks—each attempt
a brand new mistake for the birds—each
one of them experiencing the confusion
that comes along with choking

All of them sunken into the hell of comprehension—as they danced—
                        foot over foot over foot—

Docks

To my friend in the gutter:

Her voice was sweet on the phone; after hours of pacing and waiting for Gloria in the box office to appear with a tangible job. There were no crabs to be had, and no crabs to be had would mean no cranes to be pulled, and no cranes to be pulled meant no better spread of steel or spirits under rover-paned Oregon skylight.

The illusory Christmas was right around the corner, but no amount of pacing the docks would lead to a job. After having felt the grand letdown I walked back, exhausted more resources on the award-winning clam chowder and two beer bottles to drink in the van. If my boots weren't long-dragged heavy I'd have kicked myself for wandering off from my newfound sheltered charities, but with that i would have never heard her rich voice on the other line, or known the timing of the 4-4 waltz she'd teach me most nights.

Despite the docks, I followed her voice over the bridge, despite the cranes I slugged toes "home". I couldn't give a damn about the boats, I was walking for the voice on the phone.

Happy holidays my friend.

A Complicit Waltz

Something more than the sun coming up is comfortable.
Barely visible through the trees this time of year, the lesbian
couple from across the street walking their year away
alongside Golden Retriever.

Something more than reading the microwave clock is comfortable.
Using a certain shade of metropolitan vice to aid in the certain
shade of numb that experiences eyes washing back into sockets,
as sipping coffee hints at motor-skill replacement.

Something more than comfortable is the leather couch.
Decompressing limbs into the soft worn brown with rubbed-dry
spots of white where the dye faded out much like the sides
of scalp where the years wore the dimness of youth out.

Shadows dance off of tree limbs and spray across
the comfortable walls. Stretching fixes the back but
not the morning. Something else is all that life wishes
to be, dancing perhaps, blocked the leaves from all
other demands.

The Greatest Slavic Poet

I've finally uncovered the book again,
the one i've carried for more than twelve states
and booted,
collecting dust in the old trailer where Marlene and I lived.

Marlene has gone from this life,
and that is the first time I have written it on paper.

This is the first time that i've truly read the book,
it's words found me on Big Sur where if you ran carelessly in any direction
you would careen for hours, and back into your initial organic being.

The book told me to write this,
it's lines translated from Slavic
poured into another of these moments where the quiet falls under the hushed weight
of the microfine pen.

The pen acknowledged Marlene's passing
before it allowed me to,
if only because writing of such things feels like a sort of blasphemy,
a coup towards life
where everyone stands at once to shout

" We are aware of the 25th hour!"

but there is no one to shout,
there is simply the microfine pen atop Big Sur expressing these things to me.

It had nothing to say in San Francisco
where Lawrence must have paved the streets with poetic sap,
waiting to be tapped,
but alas- the sloping hills must have poured the honey south
toward the sea,
who carried it to the Slavic mouth,
and back to the pen.

The pen won't give me the great American novel,
it says these things are slow ,
and Robert Johnson has broken the credit system in hell.

My only choice now is to wait above the page,
and watch the pen do it's work,
hoping that i may contribute a few
minor notes,

But ink is contrary, and surely knows
the history of things long vibrated in throats

that never made it to

San Francisco,

the sea,

or me.

When There Were Too Many Voices For Two Ears

The moon became inherently cheese as it rolled
into that shade of orange that only July understands

There wasn't an entirely different set of colors
when I was growing up, but orange was a mistake
I was familiar with

Once, at a bus station around Queen Street, it was
an entirely different sort of affair. There was color
in sound and each person's voice carried its own
way around the rainbow

It was always interesting when there would be
distress, emotional or otherwise—it was like
talking to your mother, only her voice felt
like four entire months every time she would
finish a sentence

Digging Graves

I've never been cooler
than the day my father
left a scale packaged monster truck
on the television mantle.

The throes of childhood have a tendency
to accent the extremes,
but once;

before some things started happening,
and some things stopped happening;
I had a monster truck.

Perched atop the old cabinet television,
where I ran after finding the hornet's nest in the garage
and before having been shit on by the newly adopted kitten
in a sleeping bag
at four a.m.

Of all things on television, I remember the monster truck,
and a note,
I would write of what the note said,
but it was for me;
and I hope that there are other fathers, leaving other notes.

I remembered this around Joshua Tree
in a long train of thought that has since derailed
and jack-knifed into oblivion
(and most likely due to the federal lack of train-keeping "lucky" hobos)
but in the van,
for a second:
I remembered the monster truck.

I wonder if he knew that,
or if anyone really ever knew that time works that way,
and that time-travel is possible,

if only for a second.

Growing Back

You graduate isolation
only to return to it
some years later
        on the back patio
        at a neighbor's house
        just down the street
        and to the left

You pull yourself out of the breeze
as ashes spray from the sleeves
        of your jacket

You feel the summer
        an exodus
with each passive dusting
there in your olive green lounger

As another glass is filled
you sense the freedom
which had long escaped you
and
you sense the joy
which had shortsighted you
many years before

The sun creeps down over the line of trees
                        back in the corner
as you begin to wonder if grief will always carry
                such a hold

Directions to the job

1 Find the Wooden docks (past boat drop-in A)
2 Walk
3 Place any dreams in Jar beside job-board (adjacent to cleaning area)
4 Shake jar (try to look like you have stamina, and enough resolve to toss a cage)
5 Shake
6 Wait

Seeing Yourself In Headlights

He wondered what it meant to have something
to hear or somebody to touch

There was an ambiguous bend to his knees
            as he wondered how many hours consisted of night

The noise coming from the waffle iron more closely
resembled the phone three feet away off the hook

He stretched his legs out
            knocking into the cutlery
as he lurched across the tabletop

The highway was only a hundred feet away
and even it had drawn quiet into the night

He stood up from the table
            pressed himself against the window
gazing into the headlights in the parking lot

The sky had begun doing that sort of purple
that it does just before the sun comes or goes

He spent so much time wrapped up in himself
that he forgot the rest of it

He just stood watching the waitress and
the others outside smoking cigarettes

Much of his life was spent like his knees—always in the way
but too weak to do much of anything else

Conjunction in Midnight Blue

Zeb had a radio in the car.

The radio played the pirate station,
until it couldn't
until the FCC
and the letters on the stained porch.

The car still moved before catching fire in the mojave
and the radio played advertisements until then.

Advertisements on and on -
it opened up one day about criminality,
about the broken windows and murders,

one after the other

one after the other

"it's all a cycle" the radio said

It handed us the paperwork
to find out all about it- how the criminals work.

We were all criminals except that some of us weren't
and we were all the same citizens
except that some of us weren't
so there were no blurred lines.

Who was the judge for Oedipus
and who fired the first shot
and was it above the knee
and who stops the helicopters at three a/m
and who buries the dead.

who picks up the bullets?

We were all alive except that some of us weren't anymore.

At the end of the day the volume knob retired
and the tuner fought for naught
the radio

talked/
        talked/
and talked.

everyone believed the radio,
except that some of us didn't
and we were the criminals,

but the radio knew our names.

A Walk To The Bar

When you categorize your feet
                each step on the sidewalk feels
wrong or slightly backward

You noticed how LEDs
are on the poles now and they
                flash on and off like
the sad old man who keeps winking at your wife
                from the end of the bar

So there you are
                tired and sitting on the corner of the patio
down the street from where you started

Category is a strange fantasy
                                at this point

You can almost reflect yourself in the glass
                though
mostly you just categorize yourself into pretend
                playing along with the idea that
your feet are telling you an entirely different sort of
                empty
                        feeling

Her Twelfth Edition Art Book

The Sleep of Reason produces monsters
where there are demons under the floorboards-

While the opaque black of the Atlantic
rolls in over sky islands,
somewhere;
the artists of reason are still playing jazz music,
somewhere-the demigods of wealth
are patiently and smugly awaiting
the stone-thrower's strike
who aim leftover bullets
from every third of May,
and the ammunitions of every
muffled revolt.

IN the great cowboy west
the assailants mix vodka & orange juice
into Strbcks tmblrs
singing some Guthrie's songs
half-cocked and befuddled,
the great and soulful east
mixes molotov in Jordache's
1982 line of riot-wear.

The Sleep of Reason produces dreams,
8 hour dreams that were bled for

to Ambien caskets.

The Sleep of Reason begs the waking
to reconsider the neon night,
and escaping ground control,
and finally un-buckling as to what sort of stones
and cocktails
and notes
and rubles
need to be thrown.

The Night The Stranger Yelled At The Patio

I was sitting at a pleasant six o'clock
    the same as every table of my life.
        The patio was a pleasantry while Nate stood
            sitting straddled on his phone at nine—Daisy
                was at noon. We saw Dave pull into the lot
                    in his Porsche, though the crowd made
                      his heart uneasy I think.

                    There were people inside dancing on top
              of the bar—their drinks were dancing in their palms
      and some of them were two dollars, and some of them were nine.

    I felt some of the palms on my own as I exited through the bathroom door.

Sometimes history has a strange night at the table debating clocks in relation to friendship.

Usually you'll find me speaking there—being entirely different but entirely the same as everybody—
but on this night we found ourselves all in that same sort of unison—it was like a fire—and
        all of us were outlines of ourselves shimmering across a bar top.

The One Where Ross Leaves The Room

There is a confidence in the books that says we've done enough
bottlenecking
to keep the impressionables confined
to their respective armchairs
well-cushioned journey-[sexes]
paying alms to the sirens of industry .

There is a beauty that the books sing
in well-tailored prison displays,
the world's stories chained to bookshelves
while the pixels occupy stationary thrones
in the center of our dreams.

Save me Morpheus,
make me whole where I am lost

I wonder if I lay the phone down upon a great ceremonial altar
and set fire to

-this binary life-

if my dreams would come back to me?

Even now these lines will read incomplete.

Too Much Silent Around The Fire

There are things that I speak to myself
in line while shopping—outside while smoking—sitting
next to strangers on buses or to drivers on the
airport shuttles

Most of the time I end up figuring out how to do that with my eyes,
though most of the time is just an image that is burned into memory
—a misfortune of keyboard strokes

The level is something else entirely, something I've never developed
feelings toward, and around this fire I feel it inside of everyone

There is a grace to the social setting and it's not entirely real and it's not entirely true

Red & Black

Great casino halls of Las Vegas
The insides of the dead poet's mind.

The smell
and the sound is there
along with half-spoken memories
of some lifetime
some acquaintances.

Secret rats carry insults
and congratulations
among underground wires

[all of the dead poets must live in Valhalla now]

after whole lives of fighting
VICE&LOVE&WARS&GODS.

Vastness is there in the halls
making the poet's mind
the single worst place
to get lost
to end up

alone.

Find the madness in a roulette wheel
some Friday night
with a great renaissance devil
grinning
&
spinning the odds

Find lost
and broken
for no better hopes
of winning
or losing.

"Many of you have played here before
the things will say smiling
and history is built on columns
of dead and wailing fools
who never thought twice
to explore the poet's bones."

Those lost,
smoky catacombs of
VICE&LOVE&WARS&GODS

there where the floors try to swallow you
and walls try to crush you
you'll awake drunk
and face-down
where you've been left.

Nothing is more strange
and impressive
than the dusk
and the madness
of the poet's dream.

Lady Butcher In White

She never wore white
                    for the guests

They rode all over her for that—that butcher
                    in the kitchen

She spent her life halfway around a knife in a dress,
                    heaving small penetrations that felt more innocent
                                                    than collegiate

She always washed her hands in the brine when she was done
                    the wet webbing of her fingers stamped out the cigarettes
                    on the counter by the telephone

Suburban Home

The sea remembers anchors
falling from above,
the likeness of which we found emblazoned on our skin
        as if we ever had the right

while the not-so-proud collegiate masses
took to downtown apartments
to write essays

upon tomes of gentrification
as if in their clumsy attempts
they were wrong.

I was simply watching from the road
wondering about the whole damned thing
seeming like a game of ethnic musical chairs,
everyone scrambling for a seat
in the heart of it.

        As if we ever had the right
under the great golden
financial umbrella of law.

"now they've cornered us
now we have no place to go
now the burnt umber sea of bloodline
is spilling into every nook and cranny "

        as if we had the right.

This part of the playground
that part of the tracks
every paycheck spinning
for a hearty meal and a trinket
to keep us warm,
a sound to keep us interesting.

one hundred years ago
there was dancing around this part of town

you should've seen it
you should've been there
you should've stayed in one place

if you have it give it up,

pour it out
we may have a dollar or two to spare
some change for the subway
some credit with the cleaners.

as long as we're all chewing on the same bone
we'll keep proper company.

but don't wet it,
just lay down and have a rest

      as if any of us have the right

under the great factory-built
dome that sacrifices
what the sea remembers.

That One Part Of Thirty

No real magic in our lives this time of year,
        waking up around five to have our
        eyes wrapped around headlights
A shuffle of coffee pots stained with hard water
        in between the looks we saw in
        bathroom mirrors as we shaved
We new older timers, we new middle-age

Always feeling dicked around on the edge of sleep
        while we sort out our paychecks waiting
        in line to purchase more gasoline

3

Is anyone ready for the ring right now?
I mean out of the doorway
off of the couch
I mean into the flood
i mean out of the rain
duality in tact
sex splayed
on the front page
let me see your life
 I mean let me see it
let me see your life
I mean let me see it.

Stitch it out in print
cut it down in words
roll it up in paint
Scream it bursting into phosphorescent clouds
of bruised black glitter
on your favorite polished floor

but let us see it.

We're gonna wash it up
take it in
slide the excess
right out of your spine
are you ready?
Are you ready for the call right now?
pick up your shoes
are you ready for the world right now?
the ring
the forest and the flood
the last year
of the sun,
the last step of the road.

Solstice In Lust

We wait all of our lives inside this house
        for the spring to spring
before immediately wishing for
        something else

We tie ourselves to desire—a three legged dance—and
spread the lust over our own ideas like a butter metaphor,
hoping the future stays written—knowing we never wake up
        the same way twice

Heloise stares at us and contemplates the labor
of eating another husband

Outside sky dripping out of gutters overrun with
the two week disparity rain, painting another inconsistent
trip to the other side of noon

We sit with the corners of our eyes lit up:
        two little terrors disguised in white
        sitting on the right side of the sofa

Work

Our instincts must be inherently wrong,
it's a shame that the social conditioning;
that the advertising works so well.

We must all be helpless against the great plague
of suggested thought.

Another article on another website
at two in the afternoon
attempting to convince us (the we)
that we were simply wired incorrectly.

The children all share the fruit
If only we could share the fruit.

Fruit wasn't an ad choice in my
working-between-working window

I didn't have any choice,
If only someone would've mentioned the options.

I don't even have any fruit to share

so how is this my fault,

it must be the soldering
these fucking companies and their

click click click

brainwashing.

But i'm above it,

my wallet is the cleanest,
emptiest,
my tipping percentage is high.

I'm not one of those,
I'm not one of those,
me;
the great I.

I wish our instincts were better,
I wish that we'd had a choice.

Between The Sheet And The Direction My Mother Moved In

For a moment, each night, I would push my head
back into the mattress, trying to play temptation to the thought
that each night inside my eyelids there was exactly one pigeon

From there, I would be inside the Toronto Greyhound terminal,
and I would be stood there with the pigeon inside my eyelids,
looking for the direction of the exit, a piece of serene nature
to queue up the shadows, and I would find
the direction that my mother moved in

My sister told me right after that I would die
without a night to find myself dreaming in,
and while she was only speaking to me
in mid-announcement, only now did I begin to
think any part of that was wrong

The Heart of it All

Last night on the trip to Ohio before waking up in the wedding room,
my cousin shot a plunger full of insulin, and a snack pack of oxy into her arm.

This was in Tennessee, several hours south of the wedding room; it took place at five-
fifteen a.m. while in slept in stained-shirt and bowtie, unconscious in a river of whisky.

My mother told me on the phone before the casino

That the insulin is a sure-death
that the oxy ensures no resuscitation
it was a very specific choice.

My cousin didn't want to live here anymore.

After she changed her address the world wept and wailed,
the ex-husband who cried,
and the infant who would never gain any coming-of-age wisdom
from her only mother;

and it goes and it goes and it goes.

Sometimes things aren't good,
and you can't blame the living or the dead
in our first or last hospital rooms

for willing to do anything

for a change of scenery.

This was all, unfortunately true.

As You Situational In My Living Room

I am like you in that I'm merely desires
decorated kindly in the kinds of clothes
that make you bring somebody home with you.

I am like you in that I state intentions into windows,
playing the part of being picked apart by the savages of result.

Often I pray for an end to rain—to bitter good mornings.

I pray my intentions into the windows.

Outside, an overly-obliged spring hesitates
between cold and damp and red and orange.

I pretend there is an adamant side to life,
that I absorb everything I touch like rice in water.

You stare back as I walk in from the kitchen,
the same as myself, there are eyes in our heads
but they don't physically digest the contents.

All they see is a room and a life and that they mean the same as the other.

2

America is painting red x's on the doors,
there is something biblical about it;
like going to the barroom to pray.

Inkwells of Western canon
coming to perfect fruition
in the muddled area
between black&white
a chessboard built on half-truths.

Part One Mother Dies

Such shallow breathes and not such
                an easy way left to say anything.
There used to be so much command to taking up a room
                lighting up fires as holidays,
                or burning through stacks of letters.
Suddenly overcome by your appearance—
                how your mouth hung open
                with the dead tooth slightly catching
                        my attention.

One of your debt collectors called me for almost the entire year after.

I treated each voicemail like a phoned-in condolence.

At work I climbed into an old Pontiac
that smelled like you. I parked it in the
back row and cried for seventeen minutes.
It was an afternoon six months ago.

Then one time buying bananas at a Meijer in Hilliard
I swore you were walking fifteen feet in front of me.
I almost said your name.

There is no further walk to grief
in my sleep. I still see the letters
in your name spelled out on grocery
receipts. I hear you cackling in the
backs of movie theaters even though
I had never been to one with you.
I can't see myself where I'm going
anymore and it's not because of the
lighting on the sidewalks.

308B Trolley Car

Like why in the fuck did they build
a new taco joint uptown when
there isn't a single decent band to be heard
on Saturday night?

There's still twelve miles of aluminum stretched out broadside
stacked to the base of the peaks

LADY we need e-lectric guitar squeal and barroom identity

The bowling alley
    is a wash

    The racist bar
        is a wash

                    the wash isn't even a fucking wash

It's a trash heap renovated by tumbleweeds.

The desert killed Sam Kinnison
Like the car has been idling too long,
the kids are bored.

I'm dead, you're faking
and they built another taco joint uptown.

At least the LA smell of piss
is a constant reminder
that someone is there.

Adulting Through 21st Century

The all-encompassing "we" tells me about unhappiness.
It speaks to the sort of life that is built around missing bolts
as it traces the definitions of my face in black ink.

I have taught myself how to stop growing and it takes a toll on my legs.
I have taught myself that eventually diving breaks your neck
no matter how shallow the heart becomes in social scenes.

You become forced to lie there on the pavement beside the deep end
as you hear the ambulance approach from the west end of town.

Every week is a series of motions like this, a wheel with squared edges.

As you ride on the stretcher you want to put your face in your hands
though you cannot sit up—they have you strapped down.

You and I encounter each other in this instance and we trade wrenches.

Toe

California is a stone's throw away from Arizona,
  and a million miles in water.

It's easy to forget

that there are new rattlesnake eggs in the soil
new rocks on the mountains
new tables in the casinos
new papers in mailboxes, with their own histories.

there are new wrappers caught in the fences by the forties,
new clothes on the line
new flesh on the lake,
with new blood
flowing to new places.

There is new oil in the derricks
new warnings on the signs
new cells, in the new toe-nail
        that I stubbed in the new sun
                only to use new breath
                        in screaming at someone else's interpretation of a god.

The desert is as old as shit,

we are not.

Driving While Drowning

The shadow of the sun as a six foot three man
looming down unpainted avenue, as trees overhead
not-yet-bloomed, all the while others reminding
each of us in the car that there remained no
way for the brakes to work.

This moment, driving, all four windows cracked,
cigarettes burning in three seats, the emotions of
the afternoon seeping from the defrosting vents.

This moment, driving, telephone of the driver
ringing out some Utah area code, fifty miles
from the voice on the radio, as he adjusts
his seatbelt without a turn signal, defying the
odds of when the wheel meets the shoulder
of the person in the crosswalk.

0

There are towers of dogs in the junkyard
jutting fur upon bone
chipped tooth, ripped jowl
scratching
spine upon spine
for ascension: the rumored smell of game
long digested by ancient ancestral mouths.

They claw and climb for the idea of
scent, for the promise of tonight, and tomorrow's
and next year's supper- the security feast.

The jowl's matted blood sprays pink upon the horizon
a new sun blinding harvest red, beating down the junkyard throne
while the hounds scramble
up&up&up.

The dog no longer walks down the street.

The dog no longer graces the magazine article-

"man's best friend,
or
pursing the pooch,
or
the destinations for your pets paws"

The dogs tear toward the sky;
ambling for the keys from centuries domestication,
carrying scrimshaw the leftovers of the hunt.

Anything to gnash with teeth
in the UV burdened steel
of the rust-flavored trash heap,

just to wash out the taste,
just to cleanse the pallet.

The dog no longer walks down the street,
when the show comes to peak,
floodlights pouring on the rabbit's hide,
the fowl's leg,
let-me-in let-me-in

their hollow-bellied groans scream.

Spine upon spine
teeth upon teeth
weary from failed euthanasia
sickened from gutter-rot worms
racing
up&up&up

there are towers of dogs in the junkyard
there are towers of dogs in the junkyard
there are towers of dogs in the junkyard.

Funeral Processing

I am alone drowning in a barrel of lemonade,
sinking slowly after cutting my fins. I could see
dollar signs hovering above my children.
They were consumed in a fast fire of silent bids.

I rode an Uber over to Washington, then over
to the corner of Delaware. I was my own scene
on a frozen river—there were hunks of ice
scattered in the water as I was reprinted
into the sheets of history.

I awoke the next morning to find certain death
in the emotional debt of sinking. Hands were
leaking onto the table covered in cheeseburgers.

I was alone again, drowning again, in an
above-sea-level orphanage. My father was
lost in bottles—my mother in a jar on top of
several different dressers.

Part Two Mother Dies

These moments of sorry will come with a hug
                            or a handshake
            or a faint-of-hand shoulder touch

People will crawl out of the woodwork to give
                            you these

It'll go on so long that you'll question the very logic
            You'll begin to ask yourself if there is something else
            they're apologizing for

Eventually you realize there is

They're sorry about that—that you were born, that
you were standing in that room with the rose colored
carpeting, that a line was forming in a circle to look
at a body that was entirely your mother and entirely
was not your mother
            They're sorry that tomorrow you would have
to wake up and somehow put on pants, that you were
sitting downtown on a couch later in that day and that
the couch would be on fire
            Part of the sorry seems optimistic and genuine—
            the other half is just a frenzy of concern for
            the couch

What they don't tell you
            when somebody dies
is how many times people will walk up to you

What they don't tell you is
            how many times they'll hold your hand,
            how many times they'll look into your eyes,
            pretending to be emerged in the situation,
            how many times they'll tell you how much of
            their life was devoted to your mother—even
            though you cannot quite place them, or
            just remember them as someone who took
            Xanax from her when she was sleeping

What they don't tell you
            when somebody dies
            is how many people will walk up to you
            to tell you they're sorry—even though they
            don't understand who they're apologizing to

When We Drove Giant Winding Curve

We drove into the hallways with feet wild, abandoned to thought,
while our mother sat in a room with our father, a man she didn't quite love,
but couldn't quite leave,
and she had been pissing blood for two or three or four days

It was an elementary lesson on how to conduct traditional American holidays
        None of it at all seemed like the televisions in the florescent hallways

Valium—and its ability to silence a room—as spellbinding as
the casual lies we told the waitress on our way into town

This property of Giant Winding Curve felt entirely alien
This property of Giant Winding Curve felt entirely like last Saturday

Voices talked back to us in small huddles, around every corner,
heart monitors beeping and respirators compressing and decompressing
all along the olive and ivory tiled floors

We stared at each other until around 2:39 AM and our eyes said
most kind things
most feared things
most superimposed things
as they danced along the window line with the snow

Even as the doctor came in blundering his way through
the water pouring out—even as he talked through the
blood pouring out onto the sheets

There was pressure and movement dancing in unison
as our mother's eyes stayed locked on the wall in front of her

Sunrise Sunrise Surreal Syndicate

ONE:

Creeps down the stairway
hand in glove with cigarette
all left hand as I turn to face the
opening door

I sensed it from inside but
the cigarette smell brought it out
with further depth
—it had begun to rain

TWO:

Explorer shines in through bedroom window
slits in window shade behave as a five-bladed
razor letting sun into just the right eye

THREE:

We are all brazen with our left eyes

Still shining in the closet as the song becomes forgotten

Occasional Self Portrait

I have painted portraits of myself, as you do, as life
makes you do. Early I would pay particular attention to
form. Each aspect measured and represented and calculated
accordingly. Each leg as thin and waif as the other. I would
paint myself into a city—a landscape of truth and illusion at
the same time—myself sitting cross-legged on top of a
1991 Pontiac Grand Am—white and gray, cloth seats—this
was the place I saw in my head while I sat stoned behind the bar
in my teenage bedroom and pretended like somewhere was a place
and that then was only the present.

As time went by, I noticed much of it stayed the same
while even much more of it seemed to change. I found my
mother walking around in the background on misinterpreted
avenues. I misinterpreted her in the process. It made me swear
off ever involving myself in the art of it. I became brushes, lacquer
thinner, a waif like my legs. I realized that she would die without ever
seeing anything outside of here and the Florida coast and her family.

In my twenties there became more roots of reality or maybe
it was only trees or just the fact that trees were real. Maybe it had
something to do with responsibilities. Maybe everyone I loved
abandoned me except for my mother and my brother
and my sister and because of that I taught myself how to
alcohol properly in social settings and solitary settings. I stopped
painting cities altogether.

Then I was just in a room with a few things that at one
point held meaning. I sat at my desk and debated throwing
everything away that sat in a basket on the far corner of it.

Each of the things told their own story even though I
couldn't place a single one of them. That being the beauty
of situational garbage. Each of us act as objects that even
tell stories in silent situations. You laughed at that from
outside the room and proceeded to stare intently at the wall
until the nod came over you and a bed was presented
outside of the daytime television community. This made
you laugh even more until you decided to stick your dick
through a gloryhole only to remember that your dick wasn't
real and you retracted that entire sentiment.

I sit here now in constant threat with the glance of mirrors
adjacent to hallway closet and proceed to figure out how to
drive. I'm in the car parked behind the building I work in

refusing to accept what is about to happen to me and the fate that awaits
me beyond the immediacy of a Monday morning.

I am slightly balding. One less stroke. Occasionally the sun
plays the cards right and it's irrelevant. I am wearing gray
from head to toe and red cross trainers.

I paint these things into the portrait.

In this specific instance I feel as though I've never been
more honest but that is all entirely subjective like the
breeze or religion. Saqib is praying just fifteen feet
from my desk and a young man with a position of power is
screaming about having his cock sucked so I explain to him
where the gloryhole is located.

I am breaking apart and the only thing that matters is this
illusion and so I switch brushes. There is a truth in the action
but the action is subjective or orthodox terror and I
sigh as I try to believe the truth.

A portrait of myself—layers of glass crumbling across my
flesh, sharp bits of red as I lie in wait on the highway,
partaking the ambulance dance before the curtain calls. I
was Mount Hood from an airplane and just then I recalled
Daisy daydreaming of an interstate highway. I'm more
comfortable with these colors; swearing off the grays and
my mother coming down the side of the hill.

Technicolor Violence As Sexual Performance

She pressed into his chest
as her knees became weak,
turning her head to focus
the wallpaper into the right eye

This wasn't an exercise in concentration

This was just her way of noticing
she didn't have to take the wallpaper down

He tried very hard to swallow
—his teeth went grit for grit against themselves

She slid down to her knees
to see if it could change directions
—neither of them knew the number
of the apartment they were in

She kept her fingers around his throat,
where the numbers were

.

Corey Was Changing The Oil

ONE:

Mechanical lusting
        fluids bringing swarms
        of bees outside of bottles
        enveloped in a swarm of their own
        with questions that seemed unnecessary

In that instance, a suiter of lust the mechanic became

TWO:

There is a certain dance to pretending
        when you need to notate an ideal expression
                            of actual care

He does it with grace to the man who waits
        though not with the other that presents him bottles

This second man does not appreciate him

This second man does not see that he is a human being
        with a family and a daughter that may speak languages

THREE:

Bolts in indigo shading
        ignitions stuttering into brick walls
        exclamation lights on the instrument panel
        dinosaurs touching pistons and no reciprocation

Wife Before Dawn

There were similarities between us
but it always was a conversation revolving
around shared space that brought them out

The weekend before, she told me,
so many people ran their fingers through
her hair that she began to lose track
of her own identity

Through the tree in the yard
        the sun got placed on the other side of it

It was similar to sleep—it was silence

The kind of silence that comes out when
just enough nicotine gets into the blood to
cover up the reasons

I spent a lot of time sipping on coffee
alone in the parking lot of my job—just after 7 AM—
and like my wife—the parking lot seemed lost inside of itself

Watching Maggie Take Care Of Herself

Brushing against the edges—
it was a way to establish connection
while also reminding me as
non-physically as possible—
        she was in control,
        an entire handle made
        of the entire prior afternoon

Sheepish in her own bathing,
redundantly pulling her own arm

There was deadweight in her movements,
but there were also movements
that felt the still of roots

Brushing against the edges was symphonic

There was an automation to it,
it was something entirely done
professionally—the automation that
comes with regular practice

She knew exactly how to die
but she wouldn't bother explaining it

Fleet Only So Much

You isolate the window
pulling yourself down to
shut out the suddenly slightly
cooler Sunday

You see cars outside
and one of them is a late model
Honda Accord from the early
2000s and it has an anti-abortion
bumper sticker

The apartment warms quick
while Nate sleeps on living room floor

There are biscuits growing inside
of his gut and you know with a capital K
that it is only a consequence
of drinking too much whiskey
though we've all been there before and so
we isolate the window
              pulling ourselves down
to shut out the suddenly slightly
cooler Sunday

There is a middle-aged woman who owns
the late model Honda Accord from the early
2000s and one time when Nate didn't have biscuits
growing in his gut he told
you about seeing her go into the building
across the street at some strange hour

It was never entirely clear
the precise activity she was performing
in that building but there was a level of certainty
that the lady with the late model Honda Accord from
the early 2000s was at some sort of table with
another lady and perhaps a man and they considered
their own views
and their own windows
as they considered their own isolation
but
used up too many of their available faculties
talking about the parking space the late model Honda Accord
from the early 2000s was in

The strangeness was born out of the realization
that there were too many positions
for windows to find themselves awkward
and there carries a level of arrogance in that
and also a position of fear

This is usually why windows are left open
and only ourselves carry the isolation—the air becomes
too easy to move around unless we're lying
face down on the floor with biscuits growing
inside of our gut

Last Night Of The Microwave

I looked at myself in the mirror
for fifty-two minutes before I walked
into the kitchen and reached for the spoon drawer

I placed it in the microwave—hitting the popcorn
button—I reached down to pet Toby and went
outside for a cigarette

On the stoop I could tell that the leaves were meant to change
            and while the oak tree in the yard was some level of exceptional
it was still fully flailing and hiding under its shade
was the sad inherent tiredness that began my weekday routine

I reached into my pocket for a lighter
as I exhaled into the dust—I realized that like the
morning, I was only enough for a beginning.

Commotion Outside Apartment Window

"Apparently the Death Nail has no sympathy for weekend rest?"

"Who the fuck wakes up this early on a Saturday to hammer together
a bookshelf in a parking lot?"

These are questions they were asking
outside, as a half dozen men and
women began hammering and talking and petting the stray
cats that exist only in the Twin Coach Apartments parking
lot. There was an old man about twenty feet to their right,
around the two o'clock angle, and he had a look on his face
that clearly said he was past the comfortable stage of deciding
to yell at the hardware.

INDEX /////////////////

JUSTIN DAVID KOONTZ:

JOSHUA ROBERT LONG:

ABOUT//////////

Justin David Koontz was born into a pile of estranged dreams and comic book pages a long time ago, in the time since then there has been no short supply of ACTION, no small neglect of ADVENTURE, no discounting of the STRANGE AND BIZARRE. He grew up in some forests and creeks and city streets, a hopeful and inspired ne'er do well who chain smoked and limped along to the next lightning storm or pool hall moaning about time and time and time. He doesn't know much now aside from the true origins of questionable Japanese monster erotica, why the collective conscious loves horror movies, and the etymology of some words which he learned from books. He also knows that doom metal is better than black metal AND death metal, Triple Sec will make almost any shitty party liquor much better for a small price, Telecasters look and sound more Rock n' Roll than most other guitars, and that he loves someone called Tory (even though her true name is Terry P) and she is a truly wonderful love.

He is leaving America soon.

Instagram: @japhyrides
Facebook: facebook.com/theofficeboy
Twitter: @japhyrides
Email: aestheticbomb@gmail.com

Joshua Robert Long was born in a building that now no longer exists in Dayton, Ohio. There were some complications to the process so he did a stint in an incubator. In his teenage years he discovered the joys of no longer speaking to people and in smoking numerous cigarettes while riding in cars with the windows rolled down. By his early twenties he found himself living in Canada, which only seemed to further amplify his missing joy for the modern era of American living. He was proud that he missed out on most of the George W. Bush administration though. He currently lives in Yellow Springs, Ohio with his wife and best friend, Madeline, and their two cats.

Web: joshuarobertlong.com
Facebook: facebook.com/joshuarobertlong
Instagram: @joshuarobertlong
Twitter: @wrinkledsocks
Email: joshuarobertlong@icloud.com

WE LOVE YOU SO VERY MUCH TOBY WE JUST CANNOT SAY IT ENOUGH.

www.ingramcontent.com/pod-product-compliance
Lightning Source LLC
LaVergne TN
LVHW041326080426
835513LV00008B/608